MW00413499

Lord, Teach Us to Pray

Lord, Teach Us to Pray

A powerful, thought-provoking new look at Jesus' teaching on prayer.

ANCIL JENKINS

Gospel Advocate Company
P.O. Box 150
Nashville, Tennessee 37202

To Elaine . . .
"She brings him good . . . all the days
of his life" (Prov. 31:12)

****

IN MEMORIAM
William M. Jenkins
1896-1987
Elder, teacher of the Bible,
and teacher of how to live

Copyright © 1988 by Gospel Advocate Co.

All rights reserved. No part of this publication may be reproduced, stored in a retrieval system, or transmitted in any form or by any means—electronic, mechanical, photocopy, recording, or any other— except for brief quotations in printed reviews, without the prior permission of the publisher.

All Scripture quotations are from the New International Version, copyright © 1978, New York Bible Society. Used by permission.

Christian Communications is a division of the Gospel Advocate Co., P. O. Box 150, Nashville, TN 37202.

ISBN 0-89225-338-X

Second Printing, 1992

INTRODUCTION

I didn't write this book because I am an expert on prayer. On the contrary, I wrote it because of how little I knew on this subject. This ignorance led me to a renewed study of a subject I have often taken for granted.

This book focuses particularly on the teaching of Jesus about prayer. His life is filled with examples and lessons on the subject. Fulfilling, acceptable prayer is neither instinctive nor innate. His words and actions provide a primer to all who will learn from Him.

This book on prayer is sent forth with a prayer—that it will assist you to know Him better. To know the Master is to know how to pray.

ACKNOWLEDGMENTS

No book is ever written without the assistance of many people. The Sunset Church of Christ, Miami, Florida, was most patient as I attempted to teach these lessons. Dr. George Brown, also an author of a book on prayer, was the first to encourage me to write on this subject.

Several people read the manuscript in various stages and offered valuable suggestions. John Payne, Joe and Harriette Gray, dear friends of long standing, are among this number. Others gave encouragement when it was greatly needed.

Many thanks to Neil Anderson who kept me from wasting time on projects that were less worthy. His encouragement was constant and invaluable. Every writer should have a Don Humphrey to help them.

But most of all, to my wife Elaine, a world of gratitude for all she did. She read the manuscript at every stage. Those mistakes the computer missed, she was able to find. Above all, my thanks for her confidence in me that led me to attempt this work.

It is through the kindness and love of God's people that we can begin to comprehend His kindness and love.

CONTENTS

1

"MY HOUSE SHALL BE CALLED"

He stood to one side of the Court of the Gentiles and intently watched the happenings of commerce. In this part of the Temple area, animals for sacrifice were bought and sold. Money was changed from foreign currency into the half shekel used to pay the Temple tax. These actions were seldom quiet and not always honest. As He watched the buying and selling, the haggling and cheating, His displeasure grew.

If those who passed Him by had noticed, they might have seen Him flex an arm made strong by years of carpentry. They may have seen His fists clenched in frustration and anger. Now His eyes looked around the area, searching for something. Then, He saw it, a piece of rope that had been lost or discarded by one of the merchants. Picking it up, He doubled it, making it a whip, suitable to drive cattle out of the Temple area.

Now He quickly moved in actions that were startling and upsetting even to those involved in the clamor of the buying and selling. With a strong hand, He turned over the tables of the money changers, scattering their stacks of coins. He untied sheep and cattle and with one flick of His whip, sent them into the narrow, winding streets of Jerusalem. With a voice of authority, He commanded the sellers of birds to take them out of the Temple. As he continued His task of upsetting tables and driving out both men and animals, His voice was clearly heard above the turmoil, "My house will be called a house of prayer." *Matt 21:13; Mark 11:17; Luke 19:46.*

Centuries have passed since that spring day in Jerusalem. Yet does not our Master still observe us as He did those people? As we assemble to work and worship, doesn't He hear our prayers and observe our devotions? How do we compare to those secular-minded people whom He rebuked? Does He again feel some of the same irritation, the same disappointment, and perhaps even the same rising anger? Does He look at us and wonder, "Why have they not learned that My house is a house of prayer?"

Have the gods of this materialistic world also blinded our eyes to the power of God available to us? Have they puffed up our conceit and made us feel we have no need of prayer? Why have we not learned?

It is not because we do not know what the Bible teaches. Praying definitely occupies a place in our worship. In fact, no congregation fails to have at least two prayers at each service. Yet, there are other actions and attitudes which indicate we need to learn more about prayer and how to pray.

● It is easier to teach what prayer is not than what prayer is. We have taught much and well what the Scriptures say about God hearing sinner's prayers, about who is to lead public prayer, and how prayer is to be in Jesus' name. These are needed lessons, but there is much more that needs to be taught without leaving this undone. We need to go more to Jesus to learn what prayer is and how to pray. He both prayed and taught others how to pray. Our failure is often tragic. I read of one preacher who confessed that in sixteen years of preaching, he never preached one sermon devoted entirely to prayer.

● We have few services today that can be called "prayer meetings." Preaching the Word is the center of our worship. On occasion, the major portion of a worship service may be devoted to singing. Yet, how often is prayer the main focus of our public assembly?

Meetings for prayer need not be aided by outward trappings. Prayer rightly offered needs nothing to heighten the emotions. There is no need for select groups to meet in darkened places to have a "prayer meeting." There is power available to the church and the Christian who will pray. If we believe God can intervene today in the healing of the sick, why should we not specifically pray for this? Some have dared to begin an evangelistic service with a time of prayer for the lost. It is no surprise that souls have been saved in such efforts.

● Often prayer is a last resort. It is often said, "When all else fails, read the directions." This is defective reasoning. A person should read the directions before all else fails. We often hear requests for the church to pray for those who are critically ill or who are facing extreme difficulties. We are definitely right to do this. Jesus declared, "Again, I tell you, that if two of you on earth agree about anything you ask for, it will be done for you by my Father in heaven" (Matt. 18:19).

Since this is a very legitimate use of intercessory prayer, why wait to pray until all else has failed?

● We often hear requests from those in need of help. But how often do we hear requests for thanksgiving? It is common to hear, "Please pray for my mother as she undergoes surgery." Do we ever hear, "Please give thanks for my mother's successful surgery." We may be more anxious to ask than we are to be thankful. Is it fair to ask the Father for healing, only to give the doctors all the credit when the person recovers?

Encouragement to Pray

Prayer must begin with an awareness of our unique relationship with God. Let us not be like the prodigal son who almost starved to death because he did not fully understand his relationship with his father. God is our loving Father who delights in hearing and answering prayer. All people belong to God by right of creation. Yet there is a higher relationship reserved for His adopted children. As those who were born of Him through the water and the spirit, we can confidently call Him "Father" in the most intimate terms (see Rom. 8:15).

The beauty and strength of this relationship should be an incentive to pray. Just as a father will not ignore the requests of his children, God has promised to honor His children's intercessions (see Matt. 7:7-10). He possesses all the qualities of Fatherhood, and He combines these with His Divine knowledge of our wants, requests, and needs. We should never fail to pray because we think God does not know what we want or is not willing to grant it to us.

Our confidence in prayer is rooted in our faith in our accessibility to God. Paul told the Athenians that "He is not far from each one of us" (Acts 17:27). Jesus denounced the pagans for their much speaking in prayer. He taught, instead, of a God who is both able and willing to hear the call of His children: "For the eyes of the Lord are upon the righteous, and His ears are attentive to their prayer" (1 Pet. 3:12).

Our confidence in our access to Him cannot be based on our feelings. Sometimes people say, "I don't feel my prayers are getting through." God does not hear on this basis. Our confidence is based on our relationship with Him, not on our ability to say the right words. The Scriptures promise us He is listening if we are His children, and we may ask of Him all our needs.

Can Prayer be Learned?

God can hear us, and He will answer according to our needs, not our request. This does not minimize our need to learn more about how to pray. Our sense of need should lead us to pray. Abraham Lincoln said, "I have been driven to my knees many times by the conviction that I had no place else to go." Most people do not need to be taught they should pray. We all can learn more about how to pray.

There is One who can and will teach us. While He was on earth, people often addressed Him as "Teacher." None has been able to equal His use of methods and subject matter. Who better than Jesus to teach us how to pray?

Let us join the group of disciples who came to Him with a simple request, "Lord, teach us to pray." He is able. He is willing. He delights in seeing us come to learn of Him. *Luke 11:1*

QUESTIONS FOR DISCUSSION

1. How did the buying and selling in the Temple prevent it from being a house of prayer? What similar activities hinder our spiritual lives?

2. What changes would you like to make in your prayer life?

3. What place does prayer have where you attend church? How would you suggest it be improved?

4. Are there instances in your own life, and the lives of others, where you believe prayers have been answered?

5. How is God like an earthly father, in the matter of granting requests? How is He unlike an earthly father?

2

JESUS, MAN OF PRAYER

No one is more spiritually bankrupt than the person who needs to pray but who does not know how to approach God or what to say to Him. A cowboy once met disaster while roping a steer. The steer was so strong that he pulled the saddle off the horse, taking the cowboy with it. With his foot caught in a stirrup, the cowboy was pulled briskly across the prairie. He looked up and realized he was about to be pulled across a large bed of cactus. He later recounted that he realized he needed to pray in this predicament, but the only prayer he knew was the one he had heard others repeat before meals, "Lord, for that which we are about to receive, make us truly thankful." How often we also realize we ought to pray but we don't know how to proceed.

It was knowledge that Jesus' disciples were seeking when they asked Him to teach them to pray. However, we cannot wait until we have a complete knowledge of prayer before we begin praying. Yet we miss so much and our lives are so impoverished because we often know so little. Such knowledge enriches our spiritual life. Knowing the Father and the conditions He has set for acceptable prayer, we can find more confidence to approach Him.

Equally bankrupt is the person who knows about prayer but feels no need to seek spiritual help. It is true that disaster or tragedy often drives people to their knees. Some begin to call on God at that time. Prayer is not meant to be our emergency rations but our everyday food. Not only should we say, "Lord teach us to pray," but also, "Lord, motivate us to pray." *Luke 11: 1*

Our Motivation: the Example of Jesus

No one understood and practiced prayer as Jesus did. The place of prayer in His life is well illustrated in the gospel of Luke. Because of this gospel's many references to the devotional life of Jesus, it has often been called, "The Gospel of Prayer." Luke shows us Jesus praying on these occasions:
- At His baptism (Luke 3:21).
- When He was successful and had great crowds following Him (Luke 5;16).
- Before He chose His apostles (Luke 6:12).
- Before the feeding of the 5,000 men (Luke 9:16).
- Prior to the confession of Peter (Luke 9:18).
- On the mountain, prior to being transfigured (Luke 9:28).

- After the disciples reported their success in their preaching (Luke 10:21).
- Before His arrest in the Garden of Gethsemane (Luke 22:41-44).
- While He was on the cross (Luke 23:34).
- Before eating bread with the two disciples at Emmaus (Luke 24:30).

His disciples could clearly see the priority Jesus gave to prayer. Despite days constantly filled with ministering to those who needed Him, Jesus still had time for prayer. In the middle of constant demands for His attention, He would deliberately find time to pray. He might have to get up early. He might have to withdraw from the company of His disciples, even when they came in large numbers (Luke 5:16). He found the time to pray because He gave it the highest priority.

Absolute Necessity

We may be puzzled by this emphasis on prayer. We know Jesus was the Son of God, even God Himself in the flesh. He had come from God, and He was going back to God (John 13:3). It is not difficult to understand why human beings, such as ourselves, might be in need of much prayer. Why, however, did Jesus have such a need for prayer?

Prayer was an absolute necessity for His life. He was able to be all He was and do what He did only because of His relationship with His Father. His explanation was, "I tell you the truth, the Son can do nothing of himself" (John 5:19).

He was completely and totally human. As such, He suffered every temptation that man suffers. In fact, He endured and overcame far more than anyone else (Heb. 4:15). How was He, being human, able to overcome temptation where we fail? It was not because of His divinity. He was able to overcome and triumph over sin and the devil because of His relationship with His Father. From this communication came the strength to remain sinless.

What impact did Jesus' prayer life make on His apostles? These men saw Jesus do countless numbers of mighty works. He had healed the sick and even raised the dead in their presence. They were witnesses to the streams of people who sought Jesus' counsel. They had seen Him change a multitude of lives.

Yet, as far as we know, the apostles never asked Him to teach them how to preach, or how to work miracles, or how to help people solve problems. Yet, at least once, they came to Him and said, "Lord teach us to pray." We are not to infer they were not already praying men. They had probably been taught bedtime prayers and prayers of thanksgiving for food. These men had attended synagogue where prayers were offered. Since they had been disciples of John the Baptist, perhaps they had heard his instructions on prayer. Yet these did not meet their sense of need. They saw Jesus as the Master Teacher who knew and practiced prayer.

Luke 11:1

11

Our Knowledge: an Approachable God

Jesus brought to the Jews and the pagan world a totally new teaching. He taught of a God whom a person could approach with boldness and without fear.

The Pagan View of God. The pagan concept of deity was of gods who did not care for man. Their gods supposedly came to earth occasionally, to harass and make sport of man. If the gods had any use for man, it was solely to use him to meet their own selfish wishes. This is illustrated from the mythology of the Greeks. Prometheus aided man by giving him fire. As his punishment for being good to man, Zeus, the chief god, had Prometheus chained to a rock in the Adriatic Sea. A vulture was prepared to tear out his liver. When the vulture was finished, the liver grew back to be torn out again. This was the punishment of the god who helped man.

This view of God was demonstrated by the Stoics. Those who belonged to this pagan sect were known for their lack of emotion and their ability to bear pain without complaining. They did this because they felt they were acting like their gods. Since the gods were unfeeling, the Stoics were also unfeeling. Jesus brought these people a truth that was truly revolutionary. He taught of a God who loved and cared for man.

The Jewish View of God. The Jews of Jesus' day had a more exalted view of God. Unlike the pagans, they believed in a God who cared for man. He had demonstrated this by His deliverance of the Hebrews from Egyptian captivity and his miraculous provision for them in the wilderness.

The law of Moses, however, demonstrated a demanding God. The 613 commands of the Pentateuch set a standard that sinful man could never reach. The Jews saw Him as a God who demanded clean hands and a pure heart—no exceptions (see Ps. 24:3-5).

There is no teaching in the Old Testament of a God who could be viewed as a personal Father. Sixteen times in the Old Testament He is spoken of as Father. Yet, He is never shown as the Father of the individual, but as the Father of the nation of Israel. It seems God desired such a relationship.

Yet even in these times, God desired a deeper relationship. This truth was expressed graphically by the prophet Jeremiah:

> "How gladly would I treat you like sons, and give you a desirable land, the most beautiful inheritance of any nations! I thought you would call me 'Father' and not turn away from following Me. But like a woman unfaithful to her husband, so you have been unfaithful to me, O house of Israel" declares the Lord (Jer. 3:19-20).

How fortunate we are! Unlike the pagan, unlike the Jews under the Old Covenant, we have a relation with a God who is our personal Father (see Gal. 4:6; Rom. 8:16-17).

Jesus prayed much because of His dependence on His Father in heaven. He gave us an example to do the same.

QUESTIONS FOR DISCUSSION

1. How much have you been taught to pray? Have there been people in your life who have specifically taught you about prayer? (Mother, Father, Bible School teacher, etc.)

2. What hinders your prayer life?

3. Discuss the role of prayer in the secular world. Name some times and occasion where prayer is needed. (Example: thanksgiving for food in a public place, opening a secular meeting with prayer, etc.)

4. Relate the meaning of our lesson to this statement, "Anything worth worrying about is worth praying about."

3

"OUR FATHER"

They didn't want to interrupt Him. So they waited until they saw Him finish praying, and then they moved closer. We might wonder about their demeanor as they came to Him. Were they proud at their discovery of His strength? Did they come with downcast eyes, afraid they might be asking for something He was unwilling to give. Yet, their request was simple, "Lord, teach us to pray." Luke 11:1

We might also wonder what they expected. They might have thought He would teach them a simple, memorized prayer, as a mother would teach a child. The prayer He gave them was short, only 55 words in Matthew 6:9-13. (The version in Luke 11:2-4 is even shorter, having only 37 words.) It is a simple prayer; three out of every four words have one syllable.

Undoubtedly Jesus intended it to be more than a prayer to be recited in less than a minute. The fact that He gave us two different versions indicates He meant it to be more than this. Matthew says

He gave it as a model: "This is how you should pray" (Matt. 6:9).

"Our"

Such meaning in one simple word! This small word confines the prayer to a select group. It is not a prayer for the entire world. It was given to disciples—to those who had learned the lessons of the Beatitudes (Luke 11:1; Matthew 5:1-10). Although it is known and recited by many non-disciples, it is not intended for them. Some in the early church even used this prayer as a mark of identity in times of persecution. If a person knew this prayer, he surely was a Christian.

This word "Our" destroys the mistaken concept of a "Universal Fatherhood of God and Brotherhood of Man." Man does not approach God on the basis of his relationship with Him as a Creator but on his relationship with Him as a Father.

Although the world may reach out to God in times of stress or trial, our Father is under no obligation to answer any prayer of those who are not His children.

The word "Our" also emphasizes the community of believers. Jesus gives us a prayer with no singular pronouns. We share a common Father with all who are born again. This makes us a family. Family membership brings great privileges: "If you then, though you are evil, know how to give good gifts to your children, how much more shall your Father who is in heaven give good gifts to those who ask Him!" (Matt. 7:11).

With such a blessing comes an attendant responsibility. Jesus continued, "In everything, do to others what you have them do to you" (Matt. 7:12a).

Because God is our Father, we are to treat others as we want to be treated. Our relationships are both horizontal and vertical. Our vertical relationship is our relationship with God. Yet, with this vertical relationship, we also have a horizontal one, with our brethren and others. Both must exist. The absence of either destroys the other.

"Father"

All the best qualities of sacrifice, love, and devotion found in earthly fathers are multiplied in God. Some people have extreme difficulty in understanding the beauty and power of their relationship with their heavenly Father. Their earthly fathers exhibited few of the qualities of the heavenly Father. Martin Luther said he had great difficulty in understanding the meaning of "Our Father" because his father was stern and unyielding. If this is our difficulty, we can look to other sources to learn what the Heavenly Father is like.

Jesus showed so clearly how fathers should act toward their children:

Which of you, if his son asks for bread, will give him a stone? Or if he ask for a fish, will give him a snake? If you, then, though you are evil, know how to give good gifts to your children, how much more shall your Father in heaven give good gifts to those who ask Him! (Matt. 7:9-11).

Jesus is describing common, acceptable behavior of fathers. Anything else would be unthinkable. Even the meanest of fathers would not deny his children's request for bread. Jesus concluded, "How much more" will God do for His children? Since God is our Father, we can expect him to give us all good things.

We should be filled with comfort and hope because of the power of our Father. We need not fear that He lacks either the resources or the power to meet our needs. The Psalmist proclaimed that the earth is the Lord's and all that is in it. Haggai encouraged the Jews by reminding them that all silver and all gold belong to God (Ps. 24:1; Hag. 2:8). Paul showed us that the Father will supply our needs *according* to His riches. Since He is abundantly rich, we should expect abundant blessings.

There should be no fear that He lacks ability to answer prayer. "And God is able to make all grace abound to you" (2 Cor. 9:8). J. B. Phillips paraphrased this: "After all, God is able to give you everything you need." Our Father is both willing and able to answer our requests.

His great power is accompanied by an equal knowledge of us and our needs. He knows our needs, even better than we. Our requests to Him are not to inform Him of our needs, but to acknowledge and recognize Him as the Lord of our needs (Matt. 6:32).

In New Testament times, sparrows were considered practically worthless. They were sold two for a cent (Matt. 10:29). Yet the Father knows of every one of them. Luke gives a parallel, yet slightly different account of Jesus' words. "Are not five sparrows sold for two pennies" (Luke 12:6). Sparrows were so worthless that an extra one was thrown in if you bought two cents worth. Yet even sparrows mattered to God.

Yet God loves and cares more for us! (Matt. 6:26). His knowledge of us is just as minute, extending to the number of hairs on our head. God knows every person as an individual, not as a group. He told Cyrus that He knew him by name. (Isa. 45:3). He knows us with the same intimacy.

All of His power and knowledge would present little comfort if He did not also have great compassion for us and our needs. As a Father, God wants us to have the very best. This He is willing to provide, if we are willing to let Him be our Father.

A certain young man repeatedly got into trouble. His father patiently did whatever was necessary to pay the bills and settle his problems. A friend told the father, "If that were my boy, I would just let him go." The father replied, "I would too, if that were your boy. But, he is my son and I cannot let him go."

"In Heaven"

This part of the prayer is not intended to locate God. Everyone knows He is in heaven. Yet some people mistakenly think, "God is an old, old man who lives away in heaven." Although God is in heaven, He is not far away. In whatever dimension heaven is, He is still not far from any of us (Acts 17:27).

This phrase, "in heaven," emphasizes His holiness. He does not live on earth as we do, He is not a man as we are: "The God who made the world and everything in it is the Lord of heaven and earth and does not live in temples built by hands" (Acts 17:24).

In spite of His holiness, our Father is approachable. We are encouraged to draw near to Him, bringing our petitions to Him. Our relationship with Him is as intimate as a father with a babe. Jesus demonstrated this relationship. He used the Aramaic term, "Abba" in addressing God (Mark 14:36). This word is the first word a child learned to speak. This same intimate relationship with the Father is also granted to us (Gal. 4:6).

Many people have misunderstood this relationship. Although we have an intimate relationship, it is not a familiar, casual one. We do not address Him as "Daddy." Our closeness to Him should be greatly tempered by an appropriate understanding of His majesty. We approach Him with awe and reverence.

Conclusion

Lord Nelson, the great English admiral, once captured a ship commanded by an old acquaintance. This man was brought to Nelson's flagship to submit his sword in surrender. As he came on the ship, he saw Nelson and moved toward him with an extended hand. Nelson coldly greeted him, "First your sword, and then your hand." God our Father first asks for our surrender. Only then can a close relationship with Him become a reality.

QUESTIONS FOR DISCUSSION

1. Is there value in a memorized prayer?
2. Does God have any obligation to hear and answer the prayers of non-believers? How does one account for a seeming answer to their prayers?
3. Is there a connection between our relationship with our brethren, and our prayers being heard?
4. Is it proper to begin a prayer without addressing God as "Father"?
5. What evidence do we find in Scripture for God's care for animals?
6. How familiar can we become with God? Does familiarity erode authority?

4

"HALLOWED BE THY NAME"

Miss Watson she took me in the closet and prayed, but nothing come of it. She told me to pray every day, and whatever I asked for I would get. But it weren't so. I tried it . . . I set down one time back in the woods, and had a long think about it. I say to myself, if a body can get anything they pray for why don't Deacon Winn get back the money he lost on pork? Why can't the widow get back her silver snuff-box that was stole? . . . No, says I to myself, there ain't nothing to it.
—From *The Adventures of Huckleberry Finn* by Mark Twain

How many people have come to share Huck Finn's conclusions about prayer? Like Huck, they have prayed and have not received the proper reply to their requests. Many become disillusioned with prayer and God.

Perhaps this failure comes from an improper understanding of God. Huck Finn's problem was that his prayer was inherently selfish. He asked for himself and for his own wants. Such an immature approach is the beginning of failure in prayer.

Our first concern in prayer should not be to get what we want but to understand what God wants and what He is. The first three requests of the Model Prayer deal with God's holy name, His kingdom, and His will. The last three deal with man's most basic needs: bread, temptation, and security. It is right to pray for an ordering of events in our life, but to the end that His plans can be accomplished.

The Holy Nature of God

What does it mean for God to be "hallowed" or "holy"? Many people have difficulty with this concept because they view holiness as a negative virtue. To some people, holiness is demonstrated by what a person abstains from or refuses to do. In their view, a holy person is one who does not attend sporting events or does not wear cosmetics.

Yet holiness is part of the nature of God. It is not something He does or does not do. It is what He is. When we pray for Him to be holy, we are not praying for Him to be more of what He already is. We are praying for a better understanding of God's nature on our part. We are praying that we may understand God as He really is.

The holy nature of God is clearly taught in Scripture. The prophet Isaiah was privileged to see the throne of God with its glory and majesty. He heard God's attending servants call to one another: "Holy, Holy Holy, is the Lord Almighty; the whole earth is full of His glory" (Isa. 6:3).

The apostle John was given an even greater revelation. He was shown the throne of God in heaven. Although he gave no description of the One on the throne, he did describe the ceaseless praise given to the holiness of God: "Holy, Holy, Holy, is the Lord God Almighty, who was, and is, and is to come" (Rev. 3:8). The inhabitants of heaven are keenly aware of God's holiness and never cease to praise Him for this attribute of His nature.

What Is Holiness?

For God to be "hallowed" or "holy" is for us to understand that he is different from man. This fact is often emphasized in the Old and New Testament:

Who among the gods is like you, O Lord? Who is like you—majestic in holiness, awesome in glory, working wonders (Ex. 15:11).

For my thoughts are not your thoughts, neither are your ways my ways, declares the Lord. As the heavens are higher than the earth, so are My ways higher than your ways, and My thoughts than your thoughts (Isa. 55:8-9).

Who will not fear you, O Lord, and bring glory to your name? For you alone are holy (Rev. 15:4).

Much of the Old Testament worship and service shows the difference between God and man. The tabernacle was a tent of worship, but it was a tent far different from those man used. The priests who

24

ministered at the tabernacle were dressed differently from ordinary men. God decreed the Sabbath as a different day from other days of the week. No work at all was to be done. One purpose of the Jewish religious system was to demonstrate that God is different from man.

This is well illustrated in the life of Moses. Near the close of his leadership of the children of Israel, a need for water arose. God told Moses to speak to the rock and water would be provided. Instead, Moses chose to strike the rock and declare, "Listen, you rebels; must we bring you water out of this rock?" (Num. 20:10). He put himself on an equal footing with God in giving them water. As a result Moses lost his place in the promised land. God told Him why his punishment was so severe: "Because you did not trust in me enough to honor Me as holy in the sight of the Israelites" (Num. 20:12).

Is it possible that we may also fail to give God the honor He is due? Jesus showed us the importance of this attitude. When he told us to pray, "Hallowed by Thy name," he used the imperative mood in the Greek. The request is not punctuated with a period but with an exclamation point! Our desire to give God His rightful place in our world must be of supreme urgency to us. Like Moses, we can approach Him only when we see we are on holy ground (Ex. 3:5).

"Thy Name"

In ancient times a name stood for all that a person was. To know the "name" of God was to know His nature. When Moses asked God what His name was, he was inquiring of His nature (Ex. 3:13-14). The command, "You shall not misuse the name of the Lord your God" (Ex. 20:7), undoubtedly prohibits false swearing and profanity. Yet it also shows we are to understand who God is and to do nothing to bring Him to man's level. God is hallowed by us when we understand that He is not like man.

Our service and worship should reflect our awareness of the nature of God. Peter commands us to reverence God in our hearts as part of our preparation of giving a reason for our hope (1 Pet. 3:15). Glorifying God should be the goal of all our service and worship. The German philosopher Nietschze said, "Show me you are redeemed, and I will believe in your Redeemer."

The Results of Reverence for God

When we recognize the awesome power, knowledge, and wisdom of God, sin takes on a new meaning. When our sin is placed before a background of the love, mercy, and patience of God, it takes on horrible proportions. As long as we compare our sins only to the sins of others, they never seem very bad. William Barclay told of taking a trip by train and of being impressed by the whiteness of a small cottage. On his return trip, the ground was covered with snow. As he again passed the cottage, he saw it as dingy gray because it was surrounded by the pure, white snow. Thus do our sins take on a different color as we see them in the light of God's nature.

Sin is more than innocent mistakes. It is more than minor indiscretion. Sin is an offense against a holy, righteous, just God. David said, "Against you, and you only, I have sinned, and done what is evil in your sight" (Ps. 51:4).

The awareness of the presence of a righteous God makes a person see his own sins and inadequacies. The only result is a loathing of one's sinful condition and a desire to appear righteous before the Father (Isa. 6:5; Luke 5:8).

Understanding the holiness of God gives prayer a new, different meaning. We approach His awesome throne with our praise, thanksgiving, and requests. All our wishes are tempered with the request, "Thy will be done." We can accept all answers to all prayers because we believe an all-wise God will do what is right and best for us. In His majesty and holiness, He is not only ready and willing to hear us; He is even anxious for us to ask. This means we can come to Him with a heart of loving gratitude.

Personal Holiness Is a Lifelong Quest

Holiness is not an absolute quality. It is a quality of life which we must strive to acquire. We cannot hope for perfection—only a greater understanding of it. God wishes us to be holy because He is holy (1 Pet. 1:16).

QUESTIONS FOR DISCUSSION

1. Have you ever felt like Huck Finn when it came to prayer? How was your understanding increased?

2. How do the following statements show disrespect for God? "Just throw the trash out the window; the park doesn't belong to us." "Gosh Almighty." "What a terrible day; it is raining." "Oh God! Not again."

3. The worship and service of the Old Testament were designed to give visible evidence of the holiness of God. How is this done in New Testament service and worship?

4. What changes occurred in the lives of Isaiah and Peter as a result of their new awareness of God's nature? What can it mean to us?

5

"THY KINGDOM COME"

Living in the kingdom! How much Jesus spoke of this. It was the theme of His preaching (Mark 1:14-15). Many of His sermons were about the kingdom and what it is like to live in it (Matt. 13:25). The greatest in the kingdom, He said, was the one who became like a little child (Matt. 18:1-4). He showed us the kingdom is to be the first of our priorities (Matt. 6:33). Realizing the scope and greatness of the kingdom, is it any wonder that Jesus taught us to pray, "Thy kingdom come."

This kingdom appeared on earth on the day of Pentecost following the ascension of Jesus (Mark 9:1; Acts 1:8, 2:1ff). Does the coming of this kingdom, however, free us from also praying, "Thy kingdom come"? If we pray this, do we deny the establishment of the church on the Pentecost following the resurrection of Jesus? Some people have concluded this part of the prayer was only for the disciples in Jesus' day. We can better understand the place of this request if we broaden our knowledge of the kingdom.

What Is the "Kingdom"?

The Bible speaks of the kingdom in several different ways. It is called "the kingdom of God," "the kingdom of Christ," and "the kingdom." Jesus spoke of the kingdom as being both present and future (Luke 17:20-21; Matt. 16:28). Even after the establishment of the church, Paul taught of a future aspect of the kingdom (2 Tim. 4:18). Although the church is the kingdom of God, it is not the totality of His kingdom.

God as King. The scriptures teach of the entire creation of God as being His kingdom:

> The Lord has established His throne in heaven and His kingdom rules over all (Ps. 103:19).

> But the Lord is the true God; He is the living God, the eternal King. . . . But God made the earth by His power (Jer. 10:10-12).

As the king, God controls the world. The weather is subject to Him (Josh. 10:11: Jon. 1:4; Acts 14:17). All animals are His concern and under His control (Ps. 148:7-10). He is over the kingdoms and rulers of the earth and controls their rise and fall (Dan. 2:21,37; 4:17,25).

Although God rules the world and has all power and knowledge, not everyone recognizes this. A part of the creation does not choose to accept God's rule. Man, the crowning jewel of His creation, is in rebellion. Since man's first sin, God has worked to persuade man to accept Him as the Ruler. His desire is for man to be His willing servant. Although many will not serve Him, all will acknowledge Him one day as King. At the return of Jesus, all will bow their knee, recognizing the kingship of God and the Lordship of Christ (Phil. 2:10-11).

The Church, the Kingdom of God on Earth. To bring about God's redemption of fallen man and to ultimately bring righteous judgment on man, the kingdom of God was established on earth. All who have been born again and who have escaped from the kingdom of darkness are in this kingdom (Col. 1:13). While the kingdom is on earth, its King is in heaven (Dan. 7:13-14). Those in this kingdom have accepted the rule and sovereignty of God and His Son. This kingdom carries on the work begun by Jesus while He was on earth. It provides a light to the world and a loving, healing, forgiving fellowship to all who are part of it.

The Rule of God. The New Testament teaches another aspect of the kingdom. The word "kingdom" can refer to that which is ruled. In addition there is an abstract use in which "kingdom" refers to the authority of the ruler. Jesus referred to this when He said, "The kingdom is within you" (Luke 17:21).

> I tell you the truth, anyone who will not receive the kingdom of God like a child will never enter it (Mark 10:15).

31

The kingdom is both something we receive (the rule of God) and something we enter (the church). Jesus commanded us to "seek first the kingdom" (Matt. 6:33). The verb "seek" is in the present tense in the original language. It indicates a continual seeking. It may also be in the imperative mood. It is a command that requires urgent obedience. We must never cease desiring and searching for God's will for our lives. In this sense, we can pray for His will to "come" into our lives.

The Future Kingdom. Jesus also spoke of a future kingdom:

> When the Son of Man comes in his glory, and all the angels with him, he will sit on his throne in heavenly glory. Then the King will say to those on his right, "Come, you who are blessed by my Father, take your inheritance, the kingdom prepared for you since the creation of the world" (Matt. 25:31,34).

At the present time, the kingdom of Christ is at war with the kingdom of the devil. It is often oppressed and troubled by God's enemies (Acts 14:22). One day victory will come. Christ will appear and all His enemies will bow before Him, and His victorious kingdom will be delivered to the Father (1 Cor. 15:24).

> The kingdom of the world has become the kingdom of our Lord and of his Christ, and he will reign for ever and ever" (Rev. 11:15).

The Kingdom Is Worth Any Sacrifice

The price for citizenship is high. It makes a demand on one's priorities. Of all of these, the kingdom must be first (Matt. 6:33). When one man attempted to put his earthly father ahead of the kingdom, Jesus told him, "Let the dead bury their own dead, but you go and proclaim the kingdom of God" (Luke 9:60).

On this same occasion, another person was reluctant to follow Him. Jesus told him, "No one who has put his hand to plow and looks back is fit for service in the kingdom of God" (Luke 9:62).

Once a person is in the kingdom, he forfeits all rights to his own will. Whenever he is faced with a choice pertaining to his life, he will echo the words of Saul of Tarsus, "Lord, what will you have me do" (Acts 26:14). Such a commitment will not allow a citizen of the kingdom to make the same choices as a citizen of the world. Yet such a commitment provides great comfort and peace. By submitting to the Lord's will, a person is freed from numerous agonizing decisions.

The Invitation of Jesus

Jesus pictured His kingdom as a feast (Matt. 22:1-14; Luke 14:16-24). It is a feast to which all

33

people are invited. Some miss this feast because they do not feel it is worth very much. We must not miss this invitation by failing to see its priceless value (Luke 18-20).

What would a person be willing to give up in order to be part of this kingdom? Jesus taught and retaught this truth. One must be willing to give up everything! (Matt. 13:44-46). Never fear citizenship in the kingdom. Having God as the ruler of your life is worth whatever it costs. It caused the apostles of Jesus to say, "We have left everything and followed you" (Mark 10:28). Paul was willing to count everything as loss to gain this relationship with Christ (Phil. 3:4-8). This value is well illustrated by a person who said, "No man is a fool who gives up what he cannot keep in exchange for that which he cannot lose."

Conclusion

Can we pray for the kingdom to come? We must understand this kingdom is not to be an earthly reign of Jesus. Yet we can understand the kingdom is not only the church; it is also God's rule for our individual lives and our submission to Him. If we are in the Lord's church, we are in His kingdom. Along with being in the kingdom, we must also be striving for the kingdom, the rule of God, to become a reality in our lives. To this end, we can pray, "Thy kingdom come."

QUESTIONS FOR DISCUSSION

1. Since the entire creation of God is His kingdom, how should this affect our attitude toward our world?

2. What are the two kingdoms in our world? Discuss the blessings of membership in the Kingdom of God.

3. There are three aspects of the kingdom of God: (a) the visible, the church, (b) the personal, the kingdom within us (Luke 17:20-21); and (c) the future, heaven. Discuss how we should pray for each of these to come.

4. How does the kingdom of the world plan to overcome the Kingdom of Christ in our world?

5. What sacrifices are we called to make for the kingdom?

6

"THY WILL BE DONE"

Have you ever noted the progression of thought in Jesus' prayer? (Matt. 6:9-13). He began by addressing God ("Our Father")—the place where all prayer must begin. Then Jesus called us to a better understanding of God's nature ("Hallowed be Thy name"). He is not as man, but possesses all power, wisdom, and love. This we must respect and understand as we bring our prayers to Him.

Jesus next comes to the control of our lives. We must submit to God as our King and become a part of His kingdom. Only when we recognize this and desire Him to be in charge of our lives can we continue to pray ("Thy will be done"). At this point, we are to trust Him and His wisdom. We are ready to learn to pray, "Thy will be done."

This phrase is often misunderstood. Too often, the phrase is used in an attempt to understand the miseries and sorrows of life. Perhaps there is a tragic death in a family. Someone attempts to bring comfort by saying, "It is all for the best. The Lord's will be done." Yet this is a very incomplete attempt to understand the will of God. Being submitted to God does not mean that we will automatically accept all that life brings. Although He is in control of the world, He does not control every event of our lives.

Jesus, Our Example

Submission was the ruling principle in the life of Jesus. Although He was with God in the beginning and was Himself God, He willingly assumed the role of submission. Becoming a man, He became as we are—to the Father (John 1:1-3; Philip. 2:5-8; Heb. 5:8-9):

> My food is to do the will of Him who sent Me, and to finish His work (John 4:34).

> By myself I can do nothing; I judge only as I hear, and my judgment is just, for I seek not to please myself but him who sent me (John 5:30).

> For I have come down from heaven not to do my will but to do the will of him who sent me (John 6:38).

Jesus is the only person who ever did exactly what the Father wanted. His dedication was such that He never surrendered to His own desire.

How often we think happiness is doing exactly what we want to do. The Bible shows the falseness of this idea. It describes people who did this and were the greatest of failures. They paid a high price for such self-satisfaction. They lost their soul or their life—or both (see Judg. 14:3; **1** Sam. 25:5-11; Luke 12:16-21).

Submission Rooted in Our Concept of God

Jesus could find great joy in obedience because of His knowledge of His Father. He knew—as we should also come to know—that His Father wanted only the very best for Him. He knew if He trusted God and obeyed Him, His Father would provide all He needed (Matt. 6:33; Philip. 4:19). We are never required to understand God. We are only to understand that He is God and that He loves us.

A major danger of the humanism of our time and the resulting secular Christianity is that it glorifies man. It makes man the highest authority. Man controls his life and destiny. Thus the highest praise and glory is given man. Such a view of man can have only one result. God is taken from His throne and man is put in His place.

Let us learn that our Father is a God of love. He does everything consistent with His nature to bring about salvation. A Christian may suffer, but he can accept this as the discipline and chastening of God (Heb. 12:5-6). When a Christian accepts God's sovereignty over His life, suffering can take on purpose. Instead of asking "Why?" let us ask, "How can I find God's will in this?"

How we accept God's sovereign rule over us is important. Will we bow in humble submission or in bitter resignation. I once read of a father who asked his little girl to go on a walk with him. She did not want to, but she finally went. After they returned, the father asked, "Now, aren't you glad you decided to go along?" She replied, "I didn't decide, you were bigger than I was." May we learn to accept God's will rather than bowing to what we view as inevitable.

God's Will Can Be Hindered

All things that happen in our world are not the will of God because of the other force at work. The Bible teaches the existence of a supremely evil being. Various names are given him in the Scriptures. He is called the devil, or Satan. The book of Revelation calls him the dragon and the serpent. Each of these names tells us something about his character.

We must keep one great truth in mind. Although the devil is supernatural, he possesses only the power which God gives him. Just as God has control over mankind and gives power to the rulers of the earth, he also has control of Satan and restrains his works (Job 1:12; Isa. 44:25; Dan. 4:32; Rom. 13:1; Rev. 17:17).

This lesson is clearly taught in the book of Job. Although Job and Job's friends thought God sent the afflictions on Job, it was really the devil who tested Job. God allowed the devil to afflict Job. Yet, God set the limit of the temptation and trial. This example does not explain every reason for suffering, but it does show us that God is in control of the devil. Just as He limited his affliction of Job, He will not allow more to be added to us than we are able to bear (1 Cor. 10:12).

There is another force that can hinder God's will. It is the will of man. No person is forced to choose to serve God. Man's will can overcome God's will. Man must overcome his selfish nature before he can find the humility to allow God to be his King.

What Is the Will of God?

God's will is fully expressed in His word. The parts that are most necessary for our lives are couched in the clearest of terms. Where God has spoken, no person is entitled to an opinion. To fail to obey God's will is rebellion which will not go unpunished (see Eph. 5:17; 2 John 9).

In our personal decisions, God's will is often not clear. Decisions are faced, often daily, that demand a knowledge of God's will. Yet the Bible does not tell us where we are to live, what kind of job to take, or who to marry. How are these determined?

A knowledge of the Bible can provide help in making decisions. Although God may not clearly speak on a particular subject, the Bible contains principles that will be an adequate guide.

Personal consecration will not only cause a person to seek the will of God; it may also be a help in understanding His will. Paul spoke to this when he wrote:

> Therefore, I urge you, brothers, in view of God's mercy, to offer your bodies as living sacrifices, holy and pleasing to God—which is your spiritual worship. Do not conform any longer to the pattern of this world, but be transformed by the renewing of your mind. Then you will be able to test and approve what God's will is (Rom. 12:1-2).

Such consecration will be accompanied by humility, which will then allow a person to obey God's will.

We must be careful not to interpret our own will as the will of God. I once heard of a preacher who was invited to move to a larger congregation at a much larger salary. Someone asked his son what his father planned to do. "I don't know," the boy replied. "Pa is praying about it, and Ma is packing."

We may better understand God's will for our decisions by asking, "What would Jesus do?" Although He did not face some of the choices of our modern life, He did face temptations and decisions which were representative of these (see Heb. 4:15-16). The record of His life in the gospels shows not only His decisions but also His methods of dealing with problems and difficulties. He is our example. Let's follow His steps for wisdom (1 Pet. 2:21).

Often, common sense will tell us what we should do. If we are students of God's word and try to live as Jesus did, we will usually find an adequate basis for determining God's will.

41

"On Earth as It Is in Heaven"

Heaven is where God's will is perfectly done. John saw heaven, and he described it for us in the book of Revelation. He saw beasts, elders, and an innumerable multitude waiting anxiously to praise and glorify God. Angels were poised to do God's bidding. God desires this same attitude in His church. Take away our selfish ambitions and pretensions and many difficulties and hindrances will be eliminated from the church. The closer the church is to putting God's will first, the closer it is to being like heaven on earth.

Conclusion

Understanding the teaching on God's will should give prayer more meaning in our lives. Prayer is not an attempt to force God into submitting to our will and granting our requests. It is not presenting Him with a heavenly shopping list. Prayer is our seeking of God's will for us. It is praising Him for His majesty, wisdom, and power. It is submitting to our lot in life and striving to make it what God wants it to be. It is taking all our choices into consideration and still being able to say, "Thy will be done."

QUESTIONS FOR DISCUSSION

1. Why does the statement "It is God's will" not provide the answer to every question and happening of life?

2. Discuss the moral and spiritual problems presented by always getting your own way. Discuss some of the biblical characters who did this and what resulted.

3. Discuss this statement: "The more we trust someone, the more we will allow them to make our choices for us." Give earthly examples and also relate this to God.

4. How does God try to guide us in making our choices? What is the result if we consistently refuse such guidance?

5. Do most church difficulties arise from a failure to understand the will of God or an unwillingness of people to do God's will?

7

"GIVE US THIS DAY OUR DAILY BREAD"

The first part of prayer belongs to God! Jesus taught that His holiness, His sovereignty, and His will are to be given the prominent place in prayer. Only after these concerns are addressed should we come to God with our own needs and wishes. When we learn this arrangement of prayer, we have learned a necessary lesson in humility and are then able to receive the blessings of God.

The Request for Bread

Since our study has shown there is a logical sequence in the order of each petition in the prayer, we might think it strange that bread is the first request which man makes for himself. Why bread before forgiveness or deliverance from temptation?

The Father has promised an abundant life to His children (John 10:10). Not only does He promise this, but for this to happen His children must recognize these truths.

First, bread is man's most basic physical need. The eminent psychologist Abraham Maslow formulated a list of man's needs. He saw them as a pyramid, with the most necessary human need at the bottom. Only when this need is met is man able to begin to satisfy the next need. At the bottom of Maslow's pyramid is the need to survive. If man does not have his need for bread met, he will not be able to address the other needs.

Yet, this need is not fully met if man does not understand a basic truth—that God is the source of bread.

God is *able* to give us all we need (2 Cor. 9:8). Yet His ability does not exceed His willingness. "And my God will meet all your needs according to his glorious riches in Christ Jesus" (Philip. 4:19). A slice of bread is a powerful lesson on the grace and love of God!

The Father's concern for man's welfare is well illustrated in the life of Jesus. Jesus came to fulfill man's spiritual needs. Yet He recognized that man's physical needs also need fulfilling. He was concerned that His disciples take a rest after a period of hard work (Mark 6:31). Jesus felt compassion for a tired multitude that might faint before they got food (Matt. 15:32). After He had raised Jairus' daughter from the dead, He made certain that she was given something to eat. The breakfast that Jesus prepared for His disciples on the shore of Galilee seemed to serve only one purpose. He gave them bread and fish to make sure they had something to eat before He taught them spiritual lessons (John 21:5-10).

Daily Bread

Although scholars have produced other interpretations, there seems to be no reason to go beyond the obvious meaning of "daily bread." Jesus repeatedly taught of the Father's concern that we have bread (Matt. 6:25-26,31-34). To this end, He has always provided bread for His children. The Psalmist declared, "I was young and now I am old, yet I have never seen the righteous forsaken or their children begging bread" (Ps. 37:25).

The promised "bread" is more than white or whole wheat. It represents everything we need to live. To pray for "daily bread" is to ask God to meet our physical needs for that day.

Yet, what is needed to supply these needs may not be what we think. If a person were put on a desert island, little would be needed to sustain life. He would need water. A smaller amount of food than most of us now eat would suffice. Only enough clothes to keep us modest and maintain body temperature would be necessary. Most of us have far more than we need to live. We have come to think of our luxuries as our necessities.

Often we view our abundant possessions as evidence of the favor of God. This may be true, but our possessions may also be a mixed blessing.

46

Should we not also see them as a trial of our faith? Our abundant material goods and blessings may draw us away from putting God and His kingdom first.

> Then Jesus said to his disciples, "I tell you the truth, it is hard for a rich man to enter the kingdom of heaven. Again I tell you, it is easier for a camel to go through the eye of a needle than for a rich man to enter the kingdom of God (Matt. 19:23-26).

Riches and prosperity serve as a heavy burden. The citizen of a Third World country who has only enough to eat for one day may lack our comforts, but he may not face our temptations.

The tendency of riches is to lead us to trust in them instead of God:

> Give me neither poverty nor riches, but give me only my daily bread. Otherwise, I may have too much and disown you and say, 'Who is the Lord?' Or I may become poor and steal (Prov. 30:7-9).

The solution that Jesus gave the rich young ruler is not for us unless complete poverty is the only way to save our soul. Instead we overcome our love for riches and use them to lay up treasures in heaven (see Matt. 19:21; Luke 16:9).

"Daily Bread"

The word "daily" can be translated either as bread for today or as bread for tomorrow. In spite of the

47

debate of scholars about the exact meaning, it still refers to one day's bread.

Is not this the lesson Jesus was teaching? We are to have concern of life for one day at the time: "Therefore do not worry about tomorrow, for tomorrow will worry about itself. Each day has enough trouble of its own" (Matt. 6:34).

No finer principle for living can be found than "one day at a time." George McDonald said, "No man ever sank under the burden of the day. It is when tomorrow's burden is added to the burden of today that the load is more than man can bear." God does not promise bread for tomorrow because we are not to live tomorrow while it is still today.

This, of course, does not forbid stocking up on groceries, saving money for emergencies, or even buying life insurance. It does teach us to understand that life is so precious that it is given only one day at a time. We are to live for that day only.

"Give"

This part of the prayer is such a powerful lesson on how prayer works. Few are so naive to think if we pray, "Give us this day our daily bread," that we will find a loaf of white or whole-wheat bread on our doorstep the next morning. This phrase means that God will supply us opportunity to work, earn money, and use this to buy life's necessities. In this sense, God "gives" us our bread. God requires our cooperation in the answer to this and other prayers. He will never do for us what we can do for ourselves. In the wilderness God generously gave bread from heaven to the Israelites (see Ex. 16:15). Yet He still required them to gather the bread each day.

Our partnership with God does not require Him to do everything for us. We cannot expect God to do for us what we can do for ourselves. Under the New Covenant, God has chosen not to use miraculous, supernatural means to work in our lives. Yet He can still work in a mighty way through providential, natural means.

"Us"

There are no singular pronouns in the prayer. This does not mean that it is wrong to pray for yourself, since Jesus did this (see Matt. 26:39). It does show us we are to look beyond our own needs and desires. After our needs are met, we cannot be content if our brethren are in need (Gal. 6:10). Although our resources may be limited, we should never forget their needs and should always pray and work to meet these needs according to our ability.

Conclusion

What is the lesson of "daily bread"? It must be the same as the reason why God gave manna to the sons of Israel:

> He humbled you, causing you to hunger and then feeding you with manna, . . . to teach you that man does not live on bread alone but on every word that comes from the mouth of the Lord (Deut. 8:3).

If we believe God can provide our food and everything else we need, then we should be able to have faith that He can supply our spiritual needs in the same manner.

QUESTIONS FOR DISCUSSION

1. Why would a person ask for bread before forgiveness or deliverance from temptation?

2. How much of the riches of God do we have a right to expect God to share with us?

3. Suppose you were stranded on a desert island. What would you absolutely need to live?

4. How did Jesus try to get the rich young ruler to solve his problem with trusting riches? How much could this apply to us?

5. Read Exodus 16:13-31 about God's giving of manna to the Israelites. What parallels can you find between this passage and God's promise to supply our daily bread?

8

"FORGIVE US OUR SINS"

Although bread is to be man's first petition for himself, forgiveness is no less important. In fact, forgiveness assumes a new meaning as we note the emphasis Jesus gave it. Not only did He teach us to pray, "Forgive us our debts." He also gave additional comments on this need. He said:

> For if you forgive men when they sin against you, your heavenly Father will also forgive you. But if you do not forgive men their sins, your Father will not forgive your sins (Matt. 6:14-15).

How we need forgiveness! Just as bread is absolutely necessary to live physically, so is forgiveness necessary for our spiritual lives. Nothing compares to the burden of guilt one feels when sins are unforgiving. The Psalmist lamented, "When I kept silent, my bones wasted away through my groaning all day long. For day and night your hand was heavy upon me" (Ps. 32:3-4).

Forgiveness is necessary since we can never expect to receive what we are unwilling to give. A man once told John Wesley, "Be careful what you do, for I never forgive." Wesley replied, "Then be sure you never sin."

Yet it must be clearly understood that a prayer for forgiveness is the request of God's child. It is a prayer to the Father. This request gives no comfort to the person who has not been born again. The sinner needs complete cleansing of his past. He needs the blood of Jesus to make him clean and whole. Only then can he pray, "Forgive us our debts" (John 13:6-10). As God's children, we need not be washed again after every sin. Like Peter, we need our "feet" washed, since the whole body has already been cleansed (see John 13:6-10). We need only the forgiveness of those sins which burden us. We need only ask God and we will receive such forgiveness.

Man's Attitude Toward Sin

The great men of God have always had a deep concern for their own sinfulness. Their guilt was a heavy burden:

> For I know my transgressions, and my sin is always before me. Against you, you only, I have sinned (Ps. 51:3-4).

> When Simon Peter saw this, he fell at Jesus' knees and said, "Go away from me, Lord; I am a sinful man!" (Luke 5:8).

The great men of God not only knew their sin; they also appreciated their forgiveness. The apostle Paul truly felt the magnificence of God's forgiveness:

> I thank Christ Jesus our Lord, who . . . considered me faithful, appointing me to his service; even though I was once a blasphemer and a persecutor . . . I was shown mercy. . . . It is a trustworthy saying that deserves full acceptance: Christ Jesus came into the world to save sinners—of whom I am the worst (1 Tim. 1:12-13,15).

On the other hand, those people who refused to acknowledge their sin or even admit they had any are described in the Bible as great failures. The young man who ran to Jesus, full of excitement and interest, left with a sad face. Jesus showed his problem to be love of money. The rich young ruler did not sell everything he had because he did not admit that this sin was a problem to him (Matt. 19:16-24).

Jesus again pointed out this problem in a parable. Two men went to pray in the temple. One man, a Pharisee, prayed, "God, I thank you that I am not like all other men . . . I fast twice a week and give a tenth of all I get" (Luke 18:11-12). The other man, a tax collector, heavily burdened by his weight of sin, prayed simply, "God, have mercy on me, a sinner" (Luke 18:13).

Jesus pronounced the tax collector justified. It was not because of the length of his prayer or the goodness of his life, but because of his attitude toward himself and his sins.

This attitude leads us to seek forgiveness. The Christian does not deny his sin or even his natural tendency to be a sinful person (1 John 1:8,10). Instead, he continually confesses his individual acts of sin and finds forgiveness from God. This attitude and this confession shows us what it means to be one who is "walking in the light" (1 John 1:7-10).

"Forgive Us"

It is not hard for the righteous to recognize the sins of the world. Like righteous Lot, our souls may be tormented by the world's sensual conduct (2 Pet. 2:7-8). While our sins may not be the same as the world's, the result of living in them is the same (Isa. 59:1-2). This part of the prayer is not only an appeal for forgiveness; it is also a recognition of the horror and repugnance of sin in God's sight.

Our understanding of this idea can never let us accept a world that is lost without making an effort to change. We identify with the sinners of the world, since they are just like us. We cannot fail to love the sinners of the world, since God set an example in this regard (John 3:16).

It is easy to salve our conscience by thinking that we can do little to change the world. Yet, we cannot overlook the importance of changing one individual. To do this is to deny the power of God and our own responsibility. It does no good to moan over the conditions of our day while doing nothing to change them: "It is better to light one candle than to curse the darkness."

We often misunderstand the meaning of the concept of forgiveness. We sometimes hear, "Forgive and forget," or "I will forgive but I will never forget." Yet the human mind is such that it is incapable of forgetting anything. Thus, we must learn how we can forgive and still remember an offense.

We do have some of the capability of our Father. He speaks of putting our sins out of His sight, of putting them behind His back (Isa. 38:17). Forgiveness means that we are able to deal with people whom we have forgiven without using their offenses as the basis of our treatment of them. We do not totally forget; we just do not let our memories become part of our actions toward these people.

We cannot take comfort in an offender's refusal to repent. Jesus places an obligation on both parties. He requires the person who has hurt another to seek reconciliation with the offended party. This action is of greatest importance, even more important than worship (Matt. 5:23-24; 1 John 4:20). On the other hand, the same obligation is placed on the person who has been offended. He is to attempt to heal the misdeed. He is even to take others with him and even involve the church if necessary (Matt. 18:15-17).

Forgiveness means a restoration of the relationship that existed before the offense. This is seen so vividly in Jesus' parable of the Prodigal Son. The actions of the son broke the relationship with his father. The son eventually came to his senses. He came home and confessed his sins. Although he desired to be only a servant, the father made him a son instead. The ring, the shoes, the robe, and the calf all indicate a restoration of the love, trust, and position that had existed before the son left home (Luke 15:20-24).

The restoration of the relationship demands, however, that the offender repent and ask for forgiveness. Only on this basis can the offended forgive. When this does happen, the offended cannot refuse to forgive, even up to seventy-seven times a day (see Matt. 18:22).

"As"

"Forgive . . . as we forgive others" is one of the most solemn requests of prayer. It is a bold statement of our submission and humility. We are asking God to imitate us and our actions. We are asking Him not to forgive us if we haven't forgiven others. This does not mean a person uses forgiveness as a work of merit. It means we cannot expect to forgive what we are unwilling to give. There is no higher form of rebellion than to be unforgiving. Only the Heavenly Father knows the hearts of men and can determine whether repentance is genuine. For human beings to decide whether to forgive is to take a prerogative that belongs only to God.

How much we should adopt the spirit shown by
Joseph when his brothers asked for a reaffirmation
of his forgiveness: "Don't be afraid. Am I in the
place of God?" (Gen. 50:19).

Forgiveness is a command of God. It must be a
part of our past. We should forgive because we
have been forgiven (Col. 3:12-13). We should also
be forgiving now, as we stand in continual need of
this forgiveness (Matt. 6:13-14). Past, present and
future—we must have forgiveness.

QUESTIONS FOR DISCUSSION

1. What are some of the physical, mental, and
spiritual problems caused by unresolved guilt? How
can guilt be both good and bad for us?

2. How should you seek forgiveness of a person
who has offended you? What if this person will not
recognize his sin? What if he will not repent? How
much of this can be done if the person refuses to
repent?

3. How should you act toward a person whom
you have offended? What if he refuses to forgive?

4. How soon do we begin to trust the penitent
sinner? Is a penitent sinner disqualified from public
service in the church?

5. Is there any difference in types of sin? Are
some worse than others?

9

"LEAD US NOT INTO TEMPTATION"

Daily bread, forgiveness, deliverance from temptation—three things the Lord taught us to pray for ourselves. But suppose you could only pray for one. Which would you choose? Would you choose deliverance from temptation?

Bread is important, but it is clear that bread is not our most important priority. We also constantly need the forgiveness of God. Yet, is it not better to avoid sin than to sin and then ask God to forgive?

If we do not recognize the importance of avoiding temptation, it may be that we do not take sin very seriously. Our continual exposure to a sinful world may have blunted our awareness of sin's deception and power. Alexander Pope declared,

> Sin is a monster of such frightful mien,
> To be hated, needs only to be seen.
> But seen too oft, as face to face,
> We first pity, then endure, and then embrace.

Sin is so dangerous that we are commanded to flee from its very appearance (1 Thess. 5:22). I can remember when I was just a boy that our neighbor had a bulldog on a chain. My cousin, who was about my age, came to visit us. During the course of the afternoon, he began to tease the dog and make it angry. He knew that the dog was chained. He knew how long the chain was, so he stayed just out of the reach of the dog. What he did not know was that the dog's collar was loose. On that summer afternoon, many years ago, I saw my cousin set the unofficial world's record for the 50-yard dash!

Yet, do we not treat sin in a similar manner. Like a moth drawn to a flame, we try to get as close as possible without being consumed. Like Samson of old, we assume we can rise up and leave sin at any time we wish. This is presumptuous sin (see Ps. 19:13). Our Father has promised us a way to escape temptation (1 Cor. 10:13). Yet, we must not presume on His grace by deliberately getting as close as possible to sin.

Why Does God Allow Temptation?

Why doesn't God just destroy the devil? If temptation causes us to sin, and sin causes us to be lost, why does God not remove the source of temptation? This has been man's foolish line of reasoning for centuries. God does have the power to eliminate the devil as a force in the world. This is His ultimate plan (see Rev. 20:10).

But for God to eliminate temptation would be to make man less than he is. Our Father's ultimate plan is for man to grow into His likeness and assume His qualities (see 2 Cor. 3:18; 2 Pet. 1:4). For this to happen, man must use the knowledge that Eve and Adam gained by eating the forbidden fruit. He must know the difference between right and wrong (Gen. 2:17). With this knowledge, man has the opportunity to choose to do right.

Without this knowledge and ability, man is not man. He is merely a programmed machine. This choice is illustrated in an ancient fable. It told of the man who was given a choice of opening one of two doors. Behind one he would find a beautiful woman. Behind the other would be a tiger, waiting to attack and kill him. To get the right to choose the woman, he also had to be accept the right to choose the tiger.

Man chooses whether he will overcome or be overcome by temptation. The devil cannot overcome us and make us his servants, any more than God can. The way we meet temptation can determine our ultimate destiny. Our prayers concerning this should be of highest priority.

"Temptation"

Why would Jesus tell us to ask our Father to do the very thing He has promised not to do?

60

Lead us not into temptation (Matt. 6:13).

When tempted, no one should say, God is tempting me. For God cannot be tempted by evil, nor does he tempt anyone (Jas. 1:13).

These two Scriptures seem to present an apparent contradiction. As with other seeming biblical contradictions, the problem disappears with further knowledge and understanding. A further study shows that God does send trial or testing: "Some time later, God tested Abraham" (Gen. 22:1). In such testing, God is not inducing man to sin. Instead, the trial of our faith should be the cause of joy. It means that God is counting us worthy of being used in this way. It means He believes we are strong enough to overcome the trial and thus be made stronger.

In this you greatly rejoice, though now for a little while you may have had to suffer grief in all kinds of trials. These have come so that your faith—of greater worth than gold, which perishes even though refined by fire— may be proved genuine (1 Pet. 1:6-7).

Endure hardship as discipline; God is treating you as sons. For what son is not disciplined by his father . . . No discipline seems pleasant at the time, but painful. Later on, however, it produces a harvest of righteousness (Heb. 12:7,11).

There is a vast difference between being tested by God and being tempted to sin. Temptation produces sin and loss. Testing produces faith and strength.

Why Pray for Deliverance?

If God does not lead us into temptation, why pray for this deliverance? The meaning of Jesus is not clear. There are several possible understandings. Perhaps the best interpretation is that this phrase is a confession of our weakness and our need for God. We pray to be delivered since we know our humanity and our own tendency to sin. We believe we can overcome with God's help and that no temptation is more than we can bear. Yet, we feel it is best for us not even to face the temptation. We also admit our respect and fear of the devil. The last part of the petition supports this interpretation: "But deliver us from the evil one" (Matt. 6:13).

Some see these two petitions, "Lead us not" and "Deliver us," as being contradictory parallel expressions. The positive and negative statements are saying the same thing. Being tempted is allowing the devil, or the evil one, to come into our lives. This is a dangerous situation which we should avoid.

The Doxology

Most translations omit the doxology, "For thine is the kingdom." These words are not found in the most reliable ancient manuscripts of the New Testament. Yet, there is reason to study these words. It was traditional for Jewish prayers to end with such words of praise. Even though there is insufficient textual evidence for these exact words, there is evidence of a similar closing in some manuscripts.

To say, "Thine is the kingdom," is to ascribe to God His right to rule over us and His world. He rules His world by right of creation. He rules us by right of our regeneration.

Not only does He possess the right to be King; He also has the power. He makes His power available to His church (see Eph. 1:19-21;3:20-21). Considering His kingdom and power should drive us to our knees to give Him all the glory and praise we possess.

This prayer has no "Amen." We noted earlier that this prayer is basically an outline. "Amen" is the logical conclusion to prayer. When we say this word, it means we agree with what is said and we commit ourselves to what has been prayed. "Amen" is a statement of faith and dedication.

QUESTIONS FOR DISCUSSION

1. If God's grace is so free, why is it better to avoid sin than to sin and then seek forgiveness?

2. Although the devil is the source of temptation, what instruments does he use? What situations, people, and objects are sources of temptation to you?

3. What is the present relationship of God to the devil? How has this changed since the creation?

4. Sin can come in four stages: (a) desire, (b) opportunity, (c) temptation, and (d) involvement in sin. What can we do to stop sin at each of these stages. What can we expect God to do?

10

HOW TO GET AN ANSWER TO PRAYER

What does it take to get an answer? Some people have a very simplistic view of prayer. Often they will ask, even demand, an answer to prayer. Some of the most demanding are those who have never submitted to God in any way. A crisis or danger will drive them to pray. If their crisis passes, they may forget God until the next time they need Him. If the crisis does not pass, they blame God for not hearing them or conclude that God doesn't really exist.

The requests of some people are amazing. I read about a renowned "television evangelist" whose pet dog died suddenly. She prayed for the Lord to raise it from the dead!

But misunderstandings also exist among those who have a greater understanding of prayer. They believe prayer should include certain things. Prayer should be addressed to God as "Father." To conclude a prayer with the words, "In Jesus' Name, Amen," is certainly biblical and in harmony with the principles of prayer. Yet, it may not always be possible to pray according to this precise formula. In time of danger, grave illness, or extreme stress, we may have time only to cry, "Lord, help!"

God's hearing and answering our prayers does not always depend on our using certain words or formulas. At such time, we enjoy the help of the articulate Holy Spirit: "In the same way, the Spirit helps our weakness. We do not know what we ought to pray, but the Spirit himself intercedes for us with groans that words cannot express" (Rom. 8:26).

The Spirit carries our needs to the Father, interceding as we cannot.

God Answers All Prayers of His Children

We may be assured of two facts. First, our Father can hear all prayers. He hears them all in the sense that His great power enables Him to hear all things. Second, He answers the prayers of all His children. This is true since "No" constitutes an answer to a request. Our Father, who knows more of our needs than we, may feel that it is best for us not to receive what we ask for. He may also not give us what we want but something better instead. His wisdom may dictate that our request be delayed. Yet, our prayers are still answered:

> There is one way to always get the answer we desire. This is the assurance we have in approaching God: that

if we ask anything according to his will, he hears us
(1 John 5:14).

All requests that are within the will of God are
answered. Therefore, our concern should not be
whether God will grant our requests but whether
our requests are within His will. As we live according to His will, our prayers become more and more
in harmony with what God will grant.

What if God's Will Is Unknown?

Often we do not understand the will of God for
our lives. With personal decisions or difficulties,
we often do not understand what God wants for us.

A person can still pray boldly for these situations.
As we noted in chapter 6, there are guidelines by
which we can attempt to understand God's will for
our personal decisions. After we have determined
what seems best, we can then boldly ask for God's
answer. We need only add one phrase, "Thy will
be done." Since the devil also is allowed to work
in our world, we cannot assume that all events are
God's will. Yet the Christian has the promise that
God's will can be found in any event or happening.

If our prayers are not answered according to our
requests, we should look to the answers given.
Seek God's will in the circumstances.

It Is God's Will That We Ask in Faith

No words about prayer are more challenging than those of Jesus to His disciples:

> I tell you the truth, if anyone says to this mountain, "Go, throw yourself into the sea," and does not doubt in his heart but believes that what he says will happen, it will be done for him. Therefore I tell you, whatever you ask for in prayer, believe that you have received it, and it will be yours (Mark 11:23-24).

The only limitation Jesus placed on our prayers is the degree of our faith. He does not qualify "all things" by saying "all spiritual things." A Christian can fully ask God to move a mountain to the sea—if he is convinced that God wants the mountain moved. Although He does not restrict our requests, His teaching in other places indicate He will act only according to His will.

Our faith in prayer does not rest in our ability to say the right words. Confidence does not come from having assumed the right posture. Our confidence comes from our faith in our Father's nature, not our asking.

This seems to be the teaching of Jesus in Luke 11:5-10. He told a parable of a man who went to a friend at midnight to borrow three loaves of bread. The friend excused himself because it was inconvenient to get up. Jesus concluded, "I tell you, though he will not get up and give him the bread because he is his friend, yet because of the man's persistence he will get up and give him as much as he needs" (Luke 11:8).

Some people have understood this parable to teach that God will grant us anything if we ask often enough, long enough, and hard enough. This is not the teaching. Instead, Jesus is telling us that God, our heavenly Father, is not like the friend who would not get up. This earthly friend was persuaded by "shameless asking." Our Father is not persuaded like this. Matthew 7:7-8 does not teach us to keep on asking, seeking, and knocking until we get what we want. Instead, it teaches that as long as we keep on asking, seeking according to God's will, He will keep on giving to us.

Why Do We Not Pray More Boldly?

Since we can ask for anything that is God's will, why is there no more boldness in our prayers? Why do we not pray more boldly for the people of our world to hear the gospel? There can be no doubt that God desires the five billion people of our world to hear the gospel. Our command is to go to every creature and preach the gospel to them. Do we pray with bold confidence for this gospel to be preached and for people to accept it?

Perhaps we lack faith—not so much a lack of faith in God, but a lack of faith in ourselves. As one person said, "I don't need faith to move mountains.

I have dynamite to move mountains. I need faith to move me." When we ask God to do anything, we must not expect Him to act contrary to His nature. His nature will not allow Him to do anything for us that we can do for ourselves. When we pray for God to let all people hear the gospel, we commit ourselves to doing all we can to accomplish this task.

We often excuse our disobedience by saying, "We are not able to preach the gospel to every person." Yet, our success does not depend on our ability to accomplish something we cannot do. God is faithful to help us do all we are unable to do for ourselves. Our failure is not our lack of ability but our lack of faith in God.

Note the promise Jesus gave in Mark 11:24. After we have asked of God, we are to "believe you have received." Such confidence is ours! If we ask according to His will, the Father will answer and give what we ask.

QUESTIONS FOR DISCUSSION

1. During World War II, someone coined the phrase, "There are no atheists in foxholes." Discuss the value of prayer that is motivated by catastrophe, danger, or distress.

2. Prepare a list of Scriptural phrases that may be used to open and close prayer.

3. Discuss the role of the Holy Spirit in the inspiration of the Scriptures and His answer of our prayers. In what way are these two tasks of the Holy Spirit similar? In what ways are they different?

4. Does God answer the prayers of any people who are not His children? (see Acts 10:1-3). Does He hear and answer the prayers of His erring children?

5. Discuss this phrase, "Prayer not only reaches to God; it also motivates us."

6. Is there any request too large to bring to God?

HINDRANCES TO PRAYER

If prayer is so powerful and helpful, why is it not more important to us? Why do we not covet the prayers of others? Should it not occupy a greater and more meaningful role in our lives? Why do we not seek out causes and needs for which to pray?

The evil force in our world (the devil) does much to try to hinder our prayers. He knows the power of just one righteous person at prayer (see Jas. 5:17-18). Undoubtedly, he fears the prayers of Christians, united in common causes.

The hindrances he puts in our way to a rich prayer life are seemingly so innocent. They can be outward—the pressure of a busy life. Yet, prayer is also hindered by pride and our relationship with others.

Time Pressure

Do you have a set time for prayer? Some Christians devote a portion of their mornings for devotions. Some find the last part of the day is best. Others may have other times. Yet, to so many, time seems to be a problem. Often the morning is hectic. Evening also presents problems. A hurried life can easily distract the mind from devotion to prayer.

How did Jesus handle this? He also lived a full, busy life (see Mark 3:20). He felt constant demands from people who wished to be healed, blessed, or counseled. Yet, He found the time necessary for a full, rich life of devotion and prayer.

Jesus saw the need of a balanced life. Ministry was a priority with Him. Yet He also knew the need to balance this with times for prayer and rest. He did not let the demands of others keep him from finding time for prayer:

> Very early in the morning, while it was still dark, Jesus got up, left the house and went off to a solitary place, where he prayed (Mark 1:35).

Knowing the need for prayer, He chose to pray while others slept.

Time pressure is not so much a lack of time as a distorted sense of priority. How often we say, "I wish I had more time." There is no such thing as one person having more time than another. We all have the same amount. All hours are 60 minutes long; all days are made up of 24 hours. If some people accomplish more than others, it is probably because they have given the highest priority to what is most important.

If we neglect prayer because our days do not seem to contain enough time, our problem is not time. Jesus gave His unbroken communication with His Father His highest priority.

Despising Others

Our relationships with other people play a vital role in our prayer life. Jesus told the parable of two men who went to the temple to pray. A Pharisee, no doubt renowned for his piety, prayed, "God, I thank Thee that I am not like other people: swindlers, unjust, adulterers, or even like this tax-gatherer. I fast twice a week; I pay tithes of all I get" (Luke 18:11-12).

One writer said this man had a good eye on himself, a bad eye on his fellow man, and no eye at all on God. The Pharisee is a good illustration of the eroding, corrosive nature of pride. Pride focuses attention on self. This attention blinds a person to his fellow man. The Pharisee despised the tax collector. We can almost see a sneer on his lips as he prayed, "this tax-gatherer."

Jesus clearly taught the need for us to be in a right relationship with others before coming to worship:

> Therefore, if you are offering your gift at the altar and there remember that your brother has something against you, leave your gift there in front of the altar. First go

and be reconciled to your brother; then come and offer your gift (Matt. 5:23-24).

Although we can pray freely and ask all we need according to God's will, we need to remember that our attitude toward others affects our relationship with God. John sums up this relationship by stating that one cannot love God if he does not love his brother (1 John 4:20).

Pride also focuses on self and self-accomplishments. The Pharisee reminded God what a good servant He had. This man went to pray. He asked for nothing, received nothing, and went home worse than he was before he prayed. He had come into God's presence without being blessed. Such is the nature of pride.

Vain Repetition of Prayers

Perhaps at this stage in our study someone is thinking, "This seems too easy. All I have to do is ask according to God's will and He will give all I can ask or think." However, God's willingness to answer prayer does not relieve us of our responsibilities. Jesus also taught about the need for holiness of life.

Jesus also spoke of prayers that were "vain repetitions." "And when you pray, do not keep on babbling like pagans" (Matt. 6:7a).

Is He condemning the praying of the same thing more than once? Some have seen this as condemning the use of a memorized prayer. Yet Jesus cannot be saying that it is wrong to repeat a prayer. Three times He prayed the same prayer (Matt. 26:44). Repetition is not condemned; vain repetitions are.

What are vain repetitions? It is repeating the same prayer without thought to the meaning. It is reciting a bedtime prayer and thinking of tomorrow's tasks at the same time. Often we learn to pray from listening to others. We hear others pray about "missionaries on foreign soil," "the sick and afflicted" and the preacher's "ready recollection." We should be careful not to repeat these without giving thought to their meaning.

Prayer, both private and public, should be the sincere expression of a person's search for God's will.

Praying to Be Seen of Others

Jesus was rebuking both the present practice and the future temptation when He said, "But when you pray, do not be like the hypocrites, for they love to pray standing in the synagogues and on the street corners to be seen by men" (Matt. 6:5).

Jesus is not saying it is wrong to pray in public, nor is it wrong for people to see you pray. What is wrong is to pray solely to be seen of others. Some Pharisees gained a reputation for piety as a result of their public prayer life. They were honored and exalted. Yet Jesus condemned their action.

Those who direct prayers in public should be constantly aware of this danger. It is easy to be concerned more with the earthly listeners than the Heavenly Father. I once read of a review of a church service published by a newspaper. In commenting on the beautiful prayer, the reporter said, "It was undoubtedly one of the finest prayers ever offered to man."

Jesus gave a sober warning against those who pray with the praise of men in view: "They have received their reward in full" (Matt. 6:5b). In the original language, this phrase is a business term. It was what was written on a bill that was paid. In our terms, it means "paid in full." Jesus is saying that people who pray with the praise of others in mind will get human praise—but nothing more. This is their pay in full. The Father, who is in secret, has no further reward for them.

To overcome the danger of pride in prayer, Jesus urged us to withdraw from the world: "When you pray, go into your room, close the door and pray to your Father, who is unseen. Then your Father, who sees what is done in secret, will reward you" (Matt. 6:6). Jesus is not saying that acceptable prayer can be made only in an "inner room" or "closet." Some people live in small apartments and lack such space. Others of us have our closets so full we would never be able to get in them to pray.

Jesus is giving the antidote to pride. We should shut out the fact that people are watching and listening. Withdraw from any distraction. Keep your prayers in secret. Secret prayer brings open reward.

Conclusion

Prayer is not without its hindrances and dangers. These, however, usually come from within ourselves. If we allow ourselves to be hindered in prayer, we are also able to overcome such problems.

QUESTIONS FOR DISCUSSION

1. Discuss what can become more important than prayer.
2. What is involved in living a balanced life?
3. How much time a day should be spent in prayer?
4. Since we compliment the preacher on his sermon, should we also compliment the prayer leader on his prayer?
5. What are some of the difficulties of leading prayer in public?

12

PRAYER FOR OTHERS

"Bless all whom it is our duty to pray for." How often do we hear this or similar requests in public prayers? People who lead us in this request rightly understand there is a place in our prayers for others. Paul said, "I urge, then, first of all, that requests, prayers, intercession and thanksgiving be made for everyone" (1 Tim. 2:1).

How seriously do we take this command of God? Do we just slip in one phrase to cover this? Should we not deeply feel the needs of others?

Jesus, Our Example

Jesus both taught and practiced praying for others. Parents brought their children to Him so He might pray for them (Matt. 19:13). On the cross, He repeatedly prayed for His enemies, "Father, forgive them." In His last earthly hours, His prayer was for others (John 17). These examples indicate that intercession was surely a major part of His ministry.

The twelve apostles were often in His prayers. He told Peter, "I have prayed for you" (Luke 22:32). His prayer in John 17 is totally intercession, much of which was for the Twelve. Who can doubt that this knowledge was a source of courage and comfort to these men who led the church into all the world.

Yet, this ministry of Jesus did not end when He returned to heaven. Just as He prayed on earth for those He loved, He now continues this work: "Therefore he is able to save completely those who come to God through him, because he always lives to intercede for them" (Heb. 7:25).

What a graphic description of Jesus' continual work! Haven't you heard someone describe a devoted family man as one who "just lives for his family?" To live for something is to give it strict priority in time and concern. Jesus lives to make intercession for those who come to God through Him. His work continues.

Jesus taught us to pray for others. He showed us we should pray for others. His ascension to heaven has not stopped His work! Surely, this is an example for us.

The Power of Intercession

Does the devil ever whisper in your ear, "Your prayer won't make any difference." If you are tempted to feel this way, remember, "Elijah was a man just like us. He prayed earnestly that it would not rain, and it did not rain on the land for three and a half years. Again he prayed, and the heavens gave rain" (Jas. 5:17-18).

It is easy to dilute this power by thinking, "But that was when God was more exciting." It is true that Elijah worked miracles, but what miracle is associated with this event? God used His natural power to withhold rain. He was moved to do so by the prayer of one man.

Although we will not pray for a drought, we must realize that all the power of God is still available to us who believe (Eph. 1:19). We need not expect miracles in this stage of the Christian era. Yet, God still can use natural means to gain His ends (Acts 14:17).

As we are aware of the needs of others, they are subjects of prayer. It is our confidence that God will hear. He will answer according to His will. Although He knows, does it not make a difference if we ask and if others ask also?

The Power of United Prayer

There is power in the prayer of one person. Yet, there is even more power when believers unite in prayer: "Again, I tell you that if two of you on earth agree about anything you ask for, it will be done for you by my Father in heaven" (Matt. 18:19).

Although the context of this verse deals with withdrawing from the impenitent, the principle seems to be broader. If the church, even if it has only two or three members, can unite in prayer about anything, it will be granted. (This, of course, is if the request is according to God's will.)

It is not uncommon for the church to exercise this power in the area of sickness and distress. A serious illness will often bring a request for prayers of the church. Yet do we practice this in other areas of the Lord's work?

Our Need for Intercession

Paul was just an ordinary person. He suffered from weakness, fear, and feelings of inadequacy, just as we do. Yet, he accomplished tremendous success in spreading the gospel. There were several sources of his power. He, no doubt, prayed much. Yet, he also was encouraged, strengthened, and made bold by the prayers of others. Note how often he mentioned this.

> I urge you, brothers, by our Lord Jesus Christ and by the love of the Spirit, to join me in my struggle by praying to God for me. Pray that I may be rescued from the unbelievers in Judea (Rom. 15:30-31).
>
> On him we have set our hope that he will continue to deliver us, as you help us by your prayers (2 Cor. 1:1-11).
>
> Pray also for me, that whenever I open my mouth, words may be given to me so that I will fearlessly make known

the mystery of the gospel . . . Pray that I may declare it
fearlessly, as I should (Eph. 6:19-20).

And pray for us too, that God may open a door for our
message (Col. 4:3-4).

Brothers, pray for us (1 Thess. 5:25).

And one thing more: Prepare a guest room for me,
because I hope to be restored to you in answer to your
prayers (Phil. 22).

How much of your life is aided and strengthened
by other's praying for you? Much has been made
of the conversion of Augustine, in the fourth cen-
tury. Before his conversion, he lived a wicked,
hedonistic life. Yet, as an adult, he came to Jesus
Christ for His salvation and went on to become the
leading teacher of his day. Yet, we must not dis-
count the years of prayer his mother gave to his
soul. A friend told her, "It cannot be that a son of
so many prayers and so many tears can be lost."

What is your major source of strength? Is it your
knowledge of God and His word? Has God given
you abilities exceeding those of your brothers and
sisters? Or may your strength reside in the prayers
of others on your behalf? The knowledge of another's concern should be a mighty blow to our
pride and move us to more humility.

How much could others accomplish if we gave
more attention to intercession on their behalf? Do
you find your preacher ineffective and uninterest-
ing? How much have you prayed for him? Have
you invited several others to join with you in regular

prayer for him or for others in need of improvement and help? Prayer is so much more helpful and constructive than complaining and criticism.

The Ministry of Intercession

"Pray for me." How do you feel when someone makes this request of you? Are you shocked, embarrassed, or overwhelmed with feelings of inadequacy? These are natural reactions until we see intercession as a ministry.

How often do we feel need for the prayers of others? How great is our conviction that these petitions make a difference in our lives? Maybe we do not think of others as able ministers of intercession.

Intercession is a vital part of prayer. A vital ingredient is missing in a prayer that lacks intercession. If we forget others, we are probably too concerned with self and our needs. It is not just a coincidence there are no singular pronouns in the prayer which Jesus gave His disciples (see Matt. 6:9-13).

The President of the United States is guarded by the Secret Service. These officers wear no uniforms; they try to appear as ordinary citizens. The ministry of intercession is also a "secret service." It is a rare opportunity to serve someone without them ever knowing it. Is not this what Jesus asked us to do in prayer? Our closest prayers for others will be answered openly. They will never know what we have done, but both the pray-er and the prayed-for will be blessed.

QUESTIONS FOR DISCUSSION

1. Should a Christian have a prayer list? Does a person need to remember every person, every day, for intercession to be effective?

2. Although we would not pray for a drought, what are some things it would be good for the church to pray for in a united, specific way?

3. If you had a need, who is the first person you would call to pray for you?

4. Discuss James 5:16. What is its context? How does it relate to us? How does a Christian fulfill this command without letting someone else dominate his life?

5. What qualities are necessary for one to minister effectively through intercession for others?

13

SHALL WE FAST?

Haven't you been in a Bible class where the teacher asks for suggestions for future study? Have you noticed that fasting seems to be one of those subjects that is almost always mentioned. It is interesting there is so much interest in a subject that doesn't seem to fit with our time of indulgent luxury.

Do some people feel guilty because they have never fasted? Is it because others feel they lack something in their spiritual lives? Perhaps some have a concept of gaining the favor of God by going without food.

Fasting is definitely a New Testament subject. Jesus spoke of fasting on two occasions. Interestingly, He did not command us to fast. Instead, He approved fasting and gave regulations for this practice.

Fasting was common in the lives of many people in Jesus' day. The Law required only one day of fasting a year (see Levit. 10:29-31). The Hebrew word in this passage means to "afflict one's soul."

However, the Jews adopted other fasts (see 2 Chron. 20:3; Esth. 4:16; 2 Sam. 12:16; 1 Sam. 31:13; 1 Kings 21:9,27). By the time of Jesus, the Pharisees and others fasted often. Some fasted as often as twice a week (Luke 18:12). It had become a ritual, customary way of life. Jesus did not so much condemn their fasting as their attitude.

Fasting Must be from the Right Motive

Jesus saw much hypocrisy in the fasting of some of the people. He told the parable of the Pharisee who boasted of fasting twice a week (Luke 18:9-14). It was no coincidence that these two days were Monday and Thursday. These were the market days, when the most people could see them fast. Those fasting would put ashes on their head and wear a frown. There was a reason for this behavior. But Jesus warned against it:

> When you fast, do not look somber as the hypocrites do, for they disfigure their faces to show men they are fasting. I tell you the truth, they have received their reward in full (Matt. 6:16).

These Pharisees wanted to be seen and praised by others. This was done and the praise was given. But, this was the extent of their reward.

Jesus did not forbid their fasting or even fasting so people would know it. He did forbid fasting for the purpose of receiving human praise. He taught fasting is best kept secret to avoid any temptation of desiring human approval.

Is anyone fasting today? Really, we should not be able to find out. If Christians are following Jesus' instructions, many may be fasting but no one but them will know it!

Fasting Is Not an End Within Itself

One cannot use fasting alone to find a better standing with God. Fasting may lead us to a greater sense of devotion. Or it may be the result of service. Yet there is a danger that fasting will be completely empty and void of meaning.

Jesus condemned the outward display of religion that came from an empty heart:

> Woe to you, teachers of the law and Pharisees, you hypocrites! You are like whitewashed tombs, which look beautiful on the outside but on the inside are full of dead men's bones and everything unclean (Matt. 23:27).

Even in the Old Testament, the prophets warned of a religion that substituted fasting for righteousness and piety for justice. Isaiah told of the people asking God, "Why have we fasted, they say, as you have not seen it?" (Isa. 58:3a).

God replied:

> Yet on the day of your fasting, you do as you please and exploit all your workers. Your fasting ends in quarreling and strife, and in striking each other with wicked fists.

88

. . . Is this the kind of fast I have chosen, only a day for a man to humble himself? It is only for bowing one's head like a reed and for lying on sackcloth and ashes? . . . Is not this the kind of fasting I have chosen: to loose the chains of injustice and untie the cords of the yoke, to set the oppressed free and break every yoke? Is it not to share your food with the hungry and to provide the poor wanderer with shelter . . . when you see the naked, to clothe him (Isa. 58:3b-7).

Fasting can be a beautiful expression of service and devotion. Yet, it presents an opportunity for Satan. Weakness, self-righteousness, and pride are dangers that must be avoided (1 Cor. 7:4-6).

Reasons for Fasting

Fasting can be the result of circumstances. This is well illustrated in the life of Jesus: "Then Jesus entered a house, and again a crowd gathered, so that he and his disciples were not even able to eat" (Mark 3:20). The devotion of Jesus and His disciples to their ministry kept them so busy that there was neither time nor inclination to eat. This may be the result of service. Paul and those with him did not eat for 14 days because they were in a storm (Acts 27:33-34).

Fasting also can be the result of devotion. Our service, involvement, or prayer may mean more to us than food at times. We may wish not to be hindered by the time spent eating or be distracted by food. This type of fast can be of any length, even just one meal. A person can also abstain from certain activities or pleasures to give more time and attention to prayer or good work (1 Cor. 7:4-6).

Let us not lose our sense of perspective. We do not need to deprive ourselves of food to show God how important our prayer is to Him. He already knows. But we may use fasting to remind ourselves of the importance of prayer.

It is certainly proper to fast in order to have money to give to a good work. If a Christian has no other surplus, there is no harm in missing a meal a week or even a meal a day for a short while.

One of my professors told of an event that occurred while he was in graduate school. Shortly after the end of World War II, an appeal was made to churches for help in relieving the suffering of the people of Europe. Where this student attended church, a large amount of used clothing had been donated. He noticed his roommate had stopped eating dinner several times a week. His roommate explained his church decided to send money instead of food and clothes. Since he had no extra money, he was fasting to have some to give. We can never excuse our lack of funds for good works as long as we are willing to fast.

Conclusion

There is a place for fasting in the kingdom. Yet, it is voluntary. No one can command it of another.

On the other hand, no one has to encourage another person to stop fasting. Jesus permitted fasting, but He also gave instructions on how it should be done.

Fasting, accompanied with prayer, can be a valuable, useful tool for the Christian.

QUESTIONS FOR DISCUSSION

1. Discuss Jesus' regulations of prayer and fasting in the Sermon on the Mount. Which apply to us?

2. Is there any evidence of people today being like the Pharisees in their outward display of religion that is not accompanied by morality?

3. How can fasting be the result of circumstances? How can it be the result of devotion rather than the cause?

4. What does this statement mean to you: "Because of the nature of the kingdom, we probably need more feasting and fasting."

CPSIA information can be obtained at www.ICGtesting.com
Printed in the USA
LVOW11s1506310815

452220LV00001B/33/P